Production: N.K. Nigam

Conceived & Designed by
Pramod Kapoor
at
Roli Books CAD Centre

Fourth impression 2003

ISBN: 81-7437-068-4

Published in India by Roli Books
in arrangement with Roli & Janssen
M-75 Greater Kailash II (Market)
New Delhi 110 048, India
Ph.: (011) 29212271, 29212782, 29210886
Fax: (011) 29217185, E-mail: roli@vsnl.com
Website: rolibooks.com

Grateful thanks to **The Oberoi,** New Delhi for their
assistance in providing recipes and for making
them available for photography.

Printed and bound in Singapore

Cocktails

Dilip Chabbra

Photographs:

Dheeraj Paul

Lustre Press
Roli Books

Highball

Old-fashioned

Champagne Flute

Champagne Saucer

Brandy Snifter

White Wine

Cocktail

Long-stemmed Balloon

Beer Goblet

Sour

Long-stemmed Flute

Martini

CONTENTS

ONCE UPON A COCK-TAIL...

Time was when scruffy young men trying to mimic their gentlemanly counterparts were derisively referred to as "cocktails." The epithet derived from the name given to racing horses in England which were not thoroughbred and which were hence distinguished by having their tails "cocktailed." A mixture of spirits, called Cock-Ale, is known to have been fed to roosters just before a cockfight, and also to the winning punters, who would put as many tail feathers into their drink as the number of ingredients it contained. A ballad of 1871 which had an illustration entitled "An American Cock-Tale," sang of the tedium of the steamer ride across the Mississippi and of the tubs that would be filled with every liquor available on board, which was drunk from glasses shaped like a cock's breast and stirred with rods resembling a cock's tail.

Whatever the origin of the name, the cocktail as we know it today actually gained fame during the Prohibition Era in the United States (1920-35) where it had become customary to mix alcohol with water, sugar and bitters to hide the unpalatable flavour of the liquor then available. Necessity being the mother of all inventions, in no time at all cocktails began to surpass each other in taste and perfection. The classic favourites such as the Martini and Manhattan are products of this era.

It is generally believed that the first cocktail book was published by the Distiller's Company of London in the 17th century. Apparently though the first true book of cocktails was by Jerry Thomas who published in 1820 *The Bon Vivant's Guide* or *How to Mix Drinks.* Hence, the cocktail as a "mixed drink" has been in the lexicon of the tippler much before its fame spread across the Atlantic to Europe.

Today the term is accepted as a generic one for all mixed drinks. The cocktail bartender however, understands a cocktail to be a short drink of approximately 100 or so mls and anything larger than this would be termed a "mixed" drink or "a long drink." Since alcohol, if taken in moderation, is a useful aid to relaxation, a simple mixed drink can soothe nerves after a hard day's work. A cocktail can enliven lagging conversation, enhance a simple menu and even prod a reticent friend into garrulous outbursts.

There are a few basic and simple rules in the making of a cocktail, however, which can be easily acquired. A skilful blending of the liquids and accuracy when adding strongly flavoured ingredients are essential as even a little excess can change the flavour of the drink. This is true when adding anisette, crème de menthe and so on. Drinks with clear ingredients must be stirred while those with opaque ones like fruit juice, eggs and cream should be shaken in a cocktail shaker with rapid vertical movements. Fizzy liquids should be added only after shaking. When ice is added, it should be strained out and discarded otherwise the drink may become too diluted. While making a layered drink, tip each liquid gently on to the surface of the drink with the aid of a dessertspoon.

Ice is paramount to good mixing, for it not only chills and dilutes the drink, but also acts as a beater when the cocktail is shaken. Ice cubes are used for drinks on the rocks, shaved ice is required to create slushes, while drinks that are to be sipped with straws use crushed ice.

The glass in which the cocktail is to be served must be chosen with care so as to show off its contents to their best advantage. The shape of the glass is also important as it helps to retain the flavour of the specific drink. The rims of glasses are sometimes frosted to enhance the flavour of the drink and add a touch of exotica. To frost, dip the rim of the glass into a saucer of egg white and then into castor sugar (or lemon juice and salt, where specified). Substitute egg white with grenadine to give the frosting a pink colour.

Garnishes are added to the cocktail to enhance its flavour and to make it look attractive. Popular garnishes include seasonal fruits, cherries, orange rinds, olives, mint sprigs, cucumbers and celery sticks. Do be careful though with the quantity of garnish you use, lest your drink ends up looking like a fruit salad!

Pretty plastic straws, swizzle sticks and paper parasols give the cocktail a colourful tropical look and also come in handy for stirring or holding garnishes. So, armed with some creative instinct, some basic liquors and an appropriate glass, an ordinary homely concoction can be made to look and taste exotic.

In the following pages we have indicated some basic items you require to set up a small but well-stocked home bar. With this knowledge, the recipes in this book and a little initiative, you can make a name for yourself in the cocktail circuit in no time at all!

CHECKLIST FOR A WELL STOCKED BAR

EQUIPMENT

Barspoon
(used for stirring drinks in the mixing glass and crushing sugar and mint in some drinks).

Blender
(used for preparing drinks that require fruit to be pureed).

Boston Shaker
(used for mixing ingredients that stirring will not blend).

Measuring Cup
(used for quantities larger than 42 ml).

Jigger
(a double headed measure used for 42 ml and 21 ml or 28 and 42 ml measurements).

Mixing Glass
(used for mixing clear drinks which do not contain juices or cream).

Bottle & Can Openers
Champagne Stopper
Ice-bucket & Tongs
Ice-crusher
Citrus Fruit Reamer
Paring Knife
Pitcher
Cocktail Napkins
Lemon Juice Squeezer
Broken Cork Extractor
Toothpicks
Swizzle Sticks
Straws
Coasters

LIQUORS

Brandy (*Cognac & fruit*)
Gin
Rum (*light & dark*)
Tequila
Vodka
Whiskey *(Irish & blended)*

WINES

Campari
Champagne
Rose
Red Wine (*dry*)
Sherry (*cream & dry*)
Vermouth (*sweet & dry*)

LIQUEURS

Amaretto
Anisette
Benedictine
Cointreau
Curacao
Creme de cacao (*white & dark*)
Creme de cassis
Creme de menthe
Creme de noyaux
Drambuie
Galliano
Kahlua
Kummel
Maraschino
Sambuca (*white*)

MIXERS

Apple juice
Beer
Cola
Ginger-ale
Lime juice
Mineral water
Orange juice
Soda
Tomato juice

FLAVOURINGS

Angostura bitters
Black pepper (*ground*)
Cinnamon sticks
Cloves
Cream (*heavy & light*)
Eggs
Gomme syrup
Grated chocolate
Grenadine
Honey
Powdered nutmeg
Salt
Superfine sugar
Tabasco
Worcestershire sauce

GARNISHES

Bananas
Celery sticks
Cherries
Fresh mint sprigs
Lemon rind & slices
Olives
Orange rind & slices
Pineapple slices
Strawberries

BRANDY

Brandy, a golden spirit distilled from wine is used in such cocktails as B&B and the Brandy Cooler. Cognac and armagnac, are two best known French brandies.

Brandy's invention dates back to the 16th century. A Dutch shipmaster while transporting wine from France to Holland came up with the idea that concentrating wine by distillation prior to and adding back water after the journey, would enable him to ship more wine per trip and thus make a fortune.

Unfortunately for him, his friends tasted the concentrate before the addition of water and decided against its adulteration. They called it "brandewjin" or burnt wine which through the years got shortened to brandy.

B&B

45 ml brandy
45 ml bénédictine

Glass:
Brandy Snifter

Garnish:
None

Pour the brandy and bénédictine into the glass, stir and serve.

Cupid's Curse

30 ml brandy (Calvados)
30 ml Dubonnet
Ice cubes

Glass:
Martini

Garnish:
None

Pour both the brandy and the liqueur into a mixing glass containing 3-4 cubes of ice. Stir well, strain into the cocktail glass and serve.

Grasshopper

A popular delightful cocktail

30 ml brandy
15 ml white crème de cacao
15 ml crème de menthe
5 ml fresh lime
10 ml fresh cream

Glass:
Champagne Saucer

Garnish:
A sprig of mint

Pour all the ingredients into a Boston shaker, add 2-3 cubes of ice and shake well. Strain into the glass, add the mint sprig and serve.

Brandy Cooler

Cool and tangy as the name suggests, it will cool your heels on a hot summer's day.

45 ml brandy
90 ml apple juice
5 ml fresh lime juice
15 ml Tia Maria
Crushed ice

Glass:
Champagne Flute

Garnish:
None

Pour the first 3 ingredients into the glass in order of sequence. Add the crushed ice, float the Tia Maria on top and serve.

Brandy Alexander

An extravagant cocktail for an afternoon rendezvous.

43 ml brandy
28 ml dark crème de cacao
28 ml half-and-half (cream)
Ice cubes

Glass:
Cocktail

Garnish:
¼ tsp grated nutmeg

In a shaker half filled with ice cubes, combine the brandy, crème de cacao, and half-and-half. Shake well. Strain into the glass and serve, garnished with nutmeg.

Brandy Cobbler

56 ml brandy
84 ml club soda
5 gms superfine sugar
Crushed ice

Glass:
Old-fashioned

Garnish:
1 slice each of orange and lime and a maraschino cherry.

In the serving glass, dissolve the sugar in the club soda. Add crushed ice until the glass is almost full. Add the brandy and stir well. Serve, garnished with the orange and lime slices and cherry.

Brandy Classic

42 ml brandy
14 ml Cointreau or Triple Sec
10 ml maraschino liqueur
14 ml lemon juice
Crushed ice
15 gms castor sugar
1 lemon wedge

Glass:
Cocktail

Garnish:
None

Rub the lemon wedge on the rim of the glass and dip in the sugar to frost. In a shaker almost filled with crushed ice, combine the brandy, Cointreau, maraschino liqueur, and lemon juice. Shake well, strain into the glass and serve.

GIN

Gin, made by infusing juniper and other flavourings into a quality grain spirit is the basic ingredient in a Tom Collins and a Singapore Sling

It was first developed in the 17th century by a Dutch doctor, as a remedy for kidney ailments. The 1689 raise in excise on French wine and brandies, resulted in the cheaper gin becoming popular with the English poor.

William Hogarth, a renowned artist of the time, moved by the state of debauchery and drunkenness on gin, painted his famed picture titled "Gin Lane".

When the prohibition was lifted, gin rose to the status of a superior drink, but, it was only with the birth of the Dry Martini that gin really took off.

Gin Fizz

60 ml gin
10 ml fresh lime juice
10 ml sugar syrup
A dash of egg white
Soda as required
Ice cubes

Glass:
Highball

Garnish:
A slice of orange and cherry

Blend all the ingredients except soda with 5-6 cubes of ice. Pour straight into the glass and top with soda. Serve, garnished with half the orange slice and cherry.

Million Dollar

45 ml gin
15 ml sweet vermouth
10 ml fresh lime juice
5 ml grenadine syrup
30 ml pineapple juice
A dash of egg white
A dash of Angostura bitters
Crushed ice

Glass:
White Wine

Garnish:
A slice each of pineapple and lemon and a cherry

Pour all the ingredients into a cocktail shaker alongwith 2-3 cubes of ice and shake well. Transfer the cocktail into the glass. Serve, garnished with the pineapple and lemon slices and cherry.

Tom Collins

Another version of the "Collins", it was first made with sweetened gin, the best known brand of which was Old Tom.

60 ml gin
10 ml fresh lime juice
10 ml sugar syrup
1 bottle soda
Ice cubes

Glass:
Collins

Garnish:
A lime slice and a cherry

Pour all the ingredients into the glass alongwith 3-4 cubes of ice, top with soda and stir. Serve, garnished with the lime slice and cherry.

Dry Martini

A potent appertif, it is said to be invented for John D. Rockefeller by a bartender, Martini, at the Knickerbocker Hotel, of New York.

60 ml gin
A dash of dry vermouth
Ice cubes

Glass:
Martini

Garnish:
Stuffed olive/green olive

Pour the gin into a cocktail shaker. Add vermouth and 2-3 cubes of ice. Stir well and serve garnished with olive.

Bronx

A relic of the American Prohibition Era.

45 ml gin
15 ml dry vermouth
15 ml orange juice
15 ml fresh lime juice
A dash of egg white
Ice cubes

Glass:
Wine / Old-fashioned

Garnish:
A lime slice

Combine all the ingredients and shake vigorously alongwith the ice cubes. Strain into the wine glass (or Old-fashioned if serving on the rocks). Serve, garnished with the lime slice.

Thundering Typhoon

Bartender's own creation.

60 ml gin
30 ml orange juice
10 ml fresh lime juice
10 ml sugar syrup
A dash of egg white
Crushed ice

Glass:
Champagne Saucer

Garnish:
A slice of orange

Blend all ingredients well and serve on crushed ice. Garnish with the orange slice.

Pink Lady

A variation of the more traditional White Lady.

45 ml gin
15 ml Cointreau
10 ml fresh lime juice
5 ml pink grenadine syrup
5-10 ml fresh cream
15 gms Castor sugar

Glass:
Champagne Saucer

Garnish:
A cherry

Frost the glass using the grenadine syrup and castor sugar. Blend together all the ingredients in the blender. Strain into the glass and serve, garnished with the cherry.

Diwan-e-Khas

A tall drink, which has perhaps been derived from the ancient Indian Maharajas' recipe.

60 ml gin
10 ml sugar syrup
10 ml fresh lime juice
20 ml khus syrup
Crushed ice
2 crushed mint sprigs

Glass:
Collins/Octagonal

Garnish:
Orange segments and a mint sprig

Fill half the glass with crushed ice, add the mint and the remaining ingredients except 5 ml of khus and stir well. Fill up the glass with crushed ice and float the remaining khus syrup on top. Serve, garnished with the orange segments and sprig of mint.

Gimlet

One of the classics that has numerous variations.

60 ml gin
30 ml lime cordial
Crushed ice

Glass:
Cocktail

Garnish:
A slice of lime

Place 3 tablespoons of crushed ice in a cocktail shaker. Add the gin and lime juice and shake well. Strain into a cocktail glass. Garnish with the lime slice and serve with a pretty straw.

Flying Dutchman

A Dutch variation of the Dry Martini.

45 ml ice cold gin (Jenever)
1 tsp curaçao (Dutch)
A dash of orange bitters

Glass:
Cocktail

Garnish:
None

Put the curaçao into a chilled glass and swirl around. Empty the glass. Pour the gin, add the bitters and serve.

Skyscraper

Reminds one of a high-rise building.

45 ml gin
A dash of crème de menthe
15 ml Cointreau
15 ml fresh lime juice
10 ml sugar syrup
A dash of egg white
Crushed ice
Soda as required

Glass:
Collins

Garnish:
A slice of lime and crushed mint sprigs

Pour all the ingredients into the blender, except the soda. Blend and pour the mixture into the glass. Add crushed ice and top with soda. Serve, garnished with the lime slice and mint sprigs.

LIQUEURS

Liqueurs, delightful post dinner drinks in themselves also form the base of well-known cocktails like the Pink Squirrel, and the Grasshopper. All liqueurs are spirit based, blended with flavourings such as herbs and a sweetener. It is believed that liqueurs were first concocted as medicinal potions by ancient chemists.

As late as the 19th century, most households had their own unique blend made by adding sugar, garden herbs and fruits to local spirits.

Fruit liqueurs are either coloured (e.g. cherry brandy) or colourless. Plant liqueurs are usually colourless (eg. anisette), but take on the colour of one of the herbs used (e.g. benedictine).

Kirsch & Cassis Cooler

15 ml kirsch
45 ml crème de cassis
1 bottle soda
Ice cubes

Glass:
Brandy Balloon

Garnish:
A cherry

Mix the two liqueurs, shake with crushed ice and pour into the glass. Top with soda, 4-5 ice cubes, garnish with a cherry and serve.

Rusty Nail

A drink named after the colour of Scotch Whiskey.

30 ml whiskey (Scotch)
30 ml Drambuie
A dash of Angostura bitters

Glass:
Old-fashioned / Cocktail

Garnish:
A twist of lime

Pour the ingredients straight into the cocktail glass filled with 2-3 cubes of ice. Stir and serve garnished with the twist of lime. Use the Old-fashioned glass if serving on the rocks.

Galliano Sour

An unusual blend of whiskey and orange juice.

30 ml whiskey (Scotch)
30 ml Galliano
30 ml orange juice
½ lemon or lime juice
15 gms Castor sugar
1 lemon wedge
Ice cubes

Glass:
Cocktail

Garnish:
A slice of orange

Place 8 ice cubes in a cocktail shaker and add all the liquid ingredients. Shake well. Frost the rim of the glass using castor sugar and the lemon wedge. Strain the cocktail carefully into the glass, taking care not to disturb the frosting. Garnish with the orange slice and serve.

Vesuvio Fieroso

A drink as fiery as Mount Vesuvious.

45 ml brandy (Calvados)
15 ml orange juice
30 ml grapefruit juice
10 ml fresh lime juice
5 ml sugar syrup
Ice cubes

Glass:
Cocktail

Garnish:
Redcurrants

Pour the ingredients into a cocktail shaker alongwith 2-3 ice cubes. Shake very well and pour into the glass. Serve, garnished with the redcurrants.

Golden Cadillac

42 ml white crème de cacao
21 ml Galliano
14 ml light cream
Ice cubes

Glass:
Cocktail

Garnish:
None

In a shaker half-filled with ice cubes, combine all the ingredients. Shake well. Strain into the glass and serve.

Slique Lady

A rare mixture of vodka and kummel, to liven up your spirits.

30 ml vodka
30 ml kummel
90 ml lemonade
Crushed ice

Glass:
Sour

Garnish:
A slice of lime and a cherry

Pour the ingredients into the glass half-filled with crushed ice and top with the lemonade. Serve, garnished with the lime slice and cherry.

White Russian

A variation of Black Russian topped with fresh cream.

30 ml vodka
30 ml cafe liqueur
15 ml fresh cream
Ice cubes

Glass:
White wine

Garnish:
Chocolate flakes

Pour the vodka, liqueur and cream into the blender and blend vigorously with 2 cubes of ice. Strain into the glass. Serve, garnished with the chocolate flakes.

Pink Squirrel

42 ml crème de noyaux
14 ml white crème de cacao
28 ml light cream
Ice cubes

Glass:
Cocktail

Garnish:
None

In a shaker half-filled with ice cubes, combine all the ingredients. Shake well, strain into the glass and serve.

Apricot Sour

56 ml apricot brandy
28 ml lemon juice
1/2 teaspoon superfine sugar
Ice cubes

Glass:
Sour

Garnish:
A slice of orange and a cherry

In a shaker half-filled with ice cubes, combine the apricot brandy, lemon juice, and sugar. Shake well and strain into the glass. Serve, garnished with the orange slice and cherry.

RUM

Rum is a light, clear spirit, distilled from fermented sugarcane, matured in oakcasks and either coloured with caramel as in Jamaican or left clear as in Cuban.

It combines splendidly with other spirits, fruit juices and liquors, to form cocktails like the Pina Colada.

The name "rum" perhaps is a corruption of the word "rumbullion" meaning uproar which was used to describe a spirit drunk by the slaves working on the British West Indian plantations. In 1647, Richard Ligon's book about the islands of Barbados mentioned rum for the first time.

Around 1657, British Admiral Robert Blake, in a stroke of genius introduced the 'rum ration' in the Navy.

Pina Colada

60 ml white rum
10 ml fresh lime juice
20 ml fresh cream
20 ml coconut cream
120 ml pineapple juice
Ice cubes

Glass:
Scooped out pineapple shell / Beer Goblet

Garnish:
Cherries

Blend all the ingredients alongwith 3-4 cubes of ice so that no one ingredient is predominant. Pour the mixture into the pineapple shell and serve garnished with a few cherries.

Emerald Lily

A refreshing long drink that is perilously alcoholic.

30 ml vodka
30 ml white rum
15 ml crème de menthe
180 ml pineapple juice
15 ml fresh lime juice
A dash of egg white
Ice cubes

Glass:
Beer Goblet

Garnish:
A slice of lime and a mint sprig

Shake all the ingredients alongwith 4-5 cubes of ice. Pour it into the glass, add the garnish on the rim and serve.

Egg Nog

An ideal post-dinner drink.

30 ml rum
30 ml brandy
1 egg
Hot milk
15 ml fresh cream

Glass:
Wine

Garnish:
A pinch of cinnamon

Pour all the ingredients into the shaker and blend vigorously. Add the hot milk and stir. Pour into the glass, sprinkle with cinnamon. and serve.

Castle-in-the Air

An exotic drink after which you would keep guessing its ingredients.

45 ml dark rum
90 ml pineapple juice
20 ml coconut cream
1/2 banana (mashed)
50 ml whipped cream
Ice cubes

Glass:
Wine

Garnish:
Candied cherries

Blend the pineapple juice, coconut cream, banana and dark rum together with some ice. Pour it into the glass and float the whipped cream on top. Serve, garnished with finely chopped candied cherries.

Top Spinner

30 ml dark rum
30 ml brandy
60 ml orange juice
60 ml pineapple juice
A dash of egg white
Crushed ice

Glass:
Collins

Garnish:
A slice of orange and a cherry

Blend all the ingredients together in a blender and pour straight into the glass. Add crushed ice and stir. Serve, garnished with the orange slice and cherry.

Star Gazer

45 ml white rum
15 ml Cointreau
15 ml blue curaçao
10 ml fresh lemon juice
10 ml sugar syrup
1 bottle soda
Ice cubes

Glass:
Highball/Collins

Garnish:
A slice of lime and a cherry

Fill up the ingredients in an ice-filled glass and top with soda. Serve, garnished with the lime slice and cherry.

Tropical Melody

15 ml white rum
15 ml brandy
15 ml blue curaçao
60 ml mango juice
60 ml orange juice
10 ml fresh lime juice
Ice cubes

Glass:
Cocktail

Garnish:
A slice of pineapple, a sprig of mint and a cherry

Put all the ingredients into the shaker, add 2-3 cubes of ice and shake well. Pour into the glass, add the garnish and serve.

Chandni

Bartender's own creation.

60 ml dark rum
15 ml Cointreau
2 scoops of vanilla ice cream
300 ml cola

Glass:
Long-stemmed Flute

Garnish:
A cherry

Pour the dark rum and the vanilla ice cream into the glass. Top with cola, then float the Cointreau and serve, garnished with the cherry.

Reviver

30 ml white rum
15 ml Triple Sec
15 ml fresh lime juice
5 ml grenadine syrup

Glass:
Cocktail

Garnish:
A cherry

Blend all the ingredients and pour straight into the glass. Garnish with the cherry and serve.

Khazana

Bartender's own creation

30 ml dark rum
30 ml white rum
200 ml light black tea
(made with cloves and cinnamon)
45 ml orange juice
15 ml fresh lime juice
15 ml sugar syrup
Ice cubes

Glass:
Beer Goblet

Garnish:
A slice each of lime and orange and a cherry

Blend together all the ingredients except the tea in a blender. Pour the mixture into an ice-filled glass, add the tea and stir. Serve, garnished with the orange and lime slices and cherry.

Cuba Libra

Probably named so, when the Bacardi company left Cuba for Puerto Rico.

60 ml dark rum
300 ml cola
Ice cubes

Glass:
Highball

Garnish:
None

Pour the rum into an ice-filled glass. Top with cola and serve.

Mai Tai

The name is similar to that of a Chinese liquor, but is now a classic cocktail.

15 ml white rum
15 ml dark rum
15 ml brandy
15 ml Cointreau
10 ml fresh lime juice
10 ml sugar syrup
5 ml grenadine syrup
A dash of Angostura bitters
120 ml orange juice
Crushed ice

Glass:
Beer Goblet

Garnish:
A pineapple wedge and a cherry

Pour all ingredients except orange juice and crushed ice into the Boston Shaker and shake well. Add crushed ice and orange juice. Pour into the glass and serve, garnished with the pineapple and cherry.

Daiquiri

A classic cocktail made famous by Constante Ribalagua of La Florida restaurant, Havana, in the first half of the 20th century

42 ml light rum
28 ml lime juice
5 gms superfine sugar
Ice cubes

Glass:
Cocktail

Garnish:
None

In a shaker half-filled with ice cubes, combine the rum, lime juice and sugar. Shake well. Strain into a cocktail glass and serve.

TEQUILA

Tequila, the exclusive Mexican liquor forms a romantic base for cocktails such as Margarita, the Brave Bull and the Tequila Sunrise.

For most of the 15th century, the Mexicans, were drinking 'pulque', a low alcohol, ritual drink made from the mezcal plant. With the Spanish invasion in the 16th century, came the process of distillation of wines and tequila was born.

By the 1950s, tequila had become a favourite with the 'hip' Californians and even today it is consumed in ceremony with salt and lime in bars all over the world.

Silk Stockings

45 ml tequila
15 ml white crème de cacao
10 ml fresh cream
10 ml grenadine
15 gms castor sugar
Ice cubes

Glass:
Long-stemmed Balloon

Garnish:
None

Frost the glass with castor sugar and grenadine. Blend all the ingredients along-with 3-4 cubes of ice, strain into the glass and serve immediately.

Tequila Sunrise

The ingredients are poured straight into the glass, the grenadine providing the effect of sunrise.

45ml tequila
120 ml orange juice
5 ml grenadine syrup
Ice cubes

Glass:
Highball

Garnish:
A slice of orange

Rotate the grenadine syrup in the glass, add the ice and orange juice. Pour in the tequila and stir. Serve, garnished with the orange slice.

Caribbean Dawn

Evokes thoughts of schooners on the Caribbean Islands.

30 ml tequila
45 ml Malibu rum
1 scoop strawberry ice cream
Crushed ice

Glass:
Wine

Garnish:
A strawberry

Blend all the ingredients well and pour into the glass containing crushed ice. Serve, garnished with the strawberry.

Blue Margarita

A modern classic, said to be named after a Mexican dancer.

45 ml tequila
15 ml blue curaçao
10 ml fresh lime juice
10 ml sugar syrup
A dash of egg white
15 gms of salt
Ice cubes

Glass:
Champagne Saucer

Garnish:
A lime slice and a cherry

Frost the glass rim using salt and lime juice. Combine all the ingredients and pour into a cocktail shaker alongwith 3-4 cubes of ice. Shake well and strain into the glass. Serve, garnished with the lime slice and cherry.

General's Salute

A refreshing cocktail, which is the bartender's creation.

45 ml tequila
15 ml crème de cassis
10 ml fresh lime juice
10 ml sugar syrup
A dash of egg white
15 gms of salt
Crushed ice

Glass:
Champagne Tulip (crystal)

Garnish:
A lime slice and a cherry

Frost the rim of the glass using salt and lime juice. Shake all the ingredients well in the shaker and strain into the glass, adding crushed ice. Serve, garnished with the lime slice and cherry.

Peacock's Pride

45 ml tequila
15 ml Cointreau
150 ml cola

Glass:
Highball

Garnish:
A slice of lime and a cherry

Pour the tequila in an ice-filled glass followed by cola. Top with Cointreau and serve, garnished with the lime slice and cherry.

Mexicana

56 ml tequila
14 ml lemon juice
28 ml pineapple juice
5 ml grenadine syrup
Ice cubes

Glass:
Cocktail

Garnish:
None

In a shaker half-filled with ice cubes, combine all the ingredients. Shake well. Strain into the glass and serve.

Tequila Stinger

56 ml tequila
14 ml white crème de menthe
Ice cubes

Glass:
Cocktail

Garnish:
None

In a mixing glass half-filled with ice cubes, combine the tequila and crème de menthe. Stir well. Strain into the glass and serve.

Brave Bull

Although it's ingredients are from the Americas, this is a British recipe.

56 ml tequila
28 ml Kahlua
Ice cubes

Glass:
Old-fashioned

Garnish:
None

Pour the ingredients into the glass almost filled with ice cubes. Stir well and serve.

VODKA

Vodka was probably discovered in 14th century Russia. Origin of the word can be traced back to the Russian word "voda" meaning water.

At the onstart of World War I, the Czar of Russia incurred a ban on the production of vodka. It was legalized again only when the state took over control of all industry.

Vodka arrived in America only in the 1940s, with the Smirnoff family, thus missing the actual "cocktail boom".

Usually distilled from grain, vodka's characteristic big "kick", lack of aroma, taste and colour, makes it a versatile base for a wide range of cocktails such as the Screwdriver and Bloody Mary.

Sea Dragon

60 ml vodka
10 ml fresh lime juice
20 ml fresh cream
A piece of sweet melon (mashed)
Ice cubes

Glass:
Long-stemmed Balloon

Garnish:
A cherry

Blend all ingredients together with 3 to 4 cubes of ice and strain it into a glass. Add garnish and serve.

Torre d' Oro

"Tower of gold", it was named so probably because it gives the illusion of gold.

45 ml vodka
15 ml Cointreau
120 ml orange juice
1/2 mashed banana
15 ml fresh cream
A dash of grenadine syrup
Ice cubes

Glass:
Collins

Garnish:
Segments of seasonal fruits and a cherry

Roll the grenadine in the glass first. Blend the mashed banana, vodka and fresh cream together and pour into the glass. Add ice, pour the orange juice and stir. Pour the Cointreau on top, add the garnish and serve.

Screwdriver

Supposed to be invented by oilmen who used screwdrivers to stir the drink.

60 ml vodka
120 ml orange juice
Ice cubes

Glass:
Highball

Garnish:
A slice of orange

Pour the orange juice into an ice-filled glass, add the vodka and stir. Serve, garnished with half the orange slice.

Salty-Dog

60 ml vodka
90 ml fresh grapefruit juice
Salt to frost the glass rim
Ice cubes

Glass:
Highball

Garnish:
Grapefruit (optional)

Frost the glass rim using salt and lemon juice. Fill the glass with ice cubes, add the grapefruit juice and then the vodka, taking care to avoid damaging the salt frosting. Stir carefully and serve.

Moscow Mule

An American invention, in which you can vary the amount of vodka to adjust the "kick" of the mule.

60 ml vodka
10 ml fresh lime juice
300 ml ginger beer / ginger-ale

Glass:
Collins

Garnish:
A lime slice and mint sprigs

Pour the vodka into the glass, add the fresh lime juice and top with the ginger-ale. Serve, garnished with the lime slice and mint sprig.

Blue Lagoon

Blue drinks always add a touch of the exotic to a party. This one is no exception.

45 ml vodka
15 ml blue curaçao
10 ml fresh lime juice
10 ml sugar syrup
300 ml lemonade
Ice cubes

Glass:
Highball

Garnish:
A cherry and a orange peel spiral

Pour the ingredients into an ice-filled glass, top it up with lemonade and stir. Serve, garnished with the orange peel spiral and cherry.

Aloha

45 ml vodka
120 ml orange juice
15 ml blue curaçao
Ice cubes

Glass:
Champagne Flute

Garnish:
A slice of orange

Put 2-3 cubes of ice in the glass, add orange juice and vodka and stir. Top with blue curaçao and serve garnished with the orange slice.

Harvey Wallbanger

Named after a drunk man who collided with a wall after imbibing this drink.

30 ml vodka
60 ml orange juice
10 ml Galliano
Ice cubes

Glass:
Highball

Garnish:
A slice of orange

Place 5 ice cubes in a cocktail shaker, add the vodka and orange juice and shake well. Strain into glass, add 2 cubes of ice and float the Galliano on top. Garnish with the orange slice. and serve with a pretty straw.

Bloody Mary

It serves as a fine apertif and a morning pick-me-up.

60 ml vodka
10 ml fresh lime juice
10 ml tabasco sauce
10 ml Worcestershire sauce
A pinch of celery salt
Ice cubes
120 ml tomato juice

Glass:
Old-fashioned

Garnish:
A celery stick or a lemon wedge

Frost the glass using a lime juice and celery salt. Pour the ingredients straight into the glass in sequence, add 3-4 cubes of ice and stir. Serve, garnished with the celery stick or lemon wedge.

WHISKEY

Whiskey, distilled from fermented mash of grain and aged in wooden barrels, is believed to have originated from an anglicized version of the Gaelic word "uisgebaugh" meaning water of life.

The earliest record of spirit being distilled in Scotland is the barley-based "pot ale", probably introduced by Spanish monks at Irish religious establishments.

In 1870, the cease in cognac production and the prohibition incurred on the production of rye and bourbon in USA, resulted in a clamour for the unique flavoured Scotch.

Many countries have tried and failed to emulate the unique spring water flavour and finesse of Scotch whiskey.

Most cocktails use blended American, Irish whiskey, or Canadian whisky as a base.

Manhattan

45 ml whiskey (Bourbon)
15 ml sweet vermouth
Ice cubes

Glass:
Cocktail

Garnish:
A cherry (optional)

Stir the ingredients well, adding 2-3 cubes of ice. Strain into the glass and serve.

Tennessee

60 ml whiskey (Jack Daniels)
10 ml maraschino
10 ml lemon juice
Ice cubes

Glass:
Old-fashioned

Garnish:
A twist of lime

Combine all the ingredients and shake well alongwith 4-5 ice cubes. Pour into the glass and serve, garnished with the lime.

Rob-Roy

A popular cocktail

45 ml whiskey (Scotch)
15 ml dry vermouth
Ice cubes

Glass:
Cocktail

Garnish:
A twist of lime

Stir the ingredients with 4-5 cubes of ice and strain into the glass. Garnish with the lime and serve.

Whiskey Sour

The agreeable acidic taste makes the Sour an ideal pre-dinner drink.

60 ml whiskey (Scotch)
10 ml fresh lime juice
10 ml sugar syrup
A dash of egg white
1 dash Angostura bitters
Ice cubes

Glass:
Sour / Parfait

Garnish:
A slice of lime and a cherry

Pour all the ingredients into the blender, add 2-3 cubes of ice and blend well. Pour into the glass and serve, garnished with the lime slice and cherry.

Fine and Dandy

42 ml whiskey (Canadian)
14 ml Dubonnet
14 ml Cointreau or Triple Sec
A dash of bitters
Ice cubes

Glass:
Old-fashioned

Garnish:
A twist of lime

Combine the whiskey, Dubonnet, Cointreau and bitters in a glass almost filled with ice cubes. Serve, garnished with the lime twist.

Mint Julep

It conjurs up images of beatufiul young women of the Americas, hanging around a porch or on a swing eagerly awaiting a drink to inflame their passions.

60 ml whiskey (Bourbon)
4 sprigs of mint
5 gms castor sugar
A splash of soda/water
Crushed ice

Glass:
Collins

Garnish:
Mint sprigs

Place the sugar in a mixing glass, add 7-8 leaves of mint and mix well. Add the bourbon alongwith some soda or water and stir well, until the sugar dissolves completely. Strain and keep aside. Fill the glass with crushed ice, pour the prepared cocktail into the glass and serve, garnished with the mint sprig.

Bourbon Old-fashioned

The whiskey must be American, preferably Jack Daniels.

60 ml whiskey (Bourbon)
A dash of Angostura bitters
1 cube of sugar
60 ml soda
Ice cubes

Glass:
Old-fashioned

Garnish:
A slice each of lime and orange and a cherry

Stir all the ingredients and serve it on the rocks. Garnish with the orange and lime slices and cherry.

New Yorker

For those who enjoy their drinks slightly sweet.

60 ml whiskey (Bourbon)
15 ml lime juice
A dash of grenadine syrup
Ice cubes

Glass:
Cocktail

Garnish:
A twist of orange peel

Shake the bourbon, lime juice, grenadine syrup and ice cubes together in a shaker. Strain and pour into the glass. Serve, garnished with the orange peel.

Perfect Manhattan

It is a variation of Dry Manhattan using the same amount of vermouth but half Italian sweet and half French dry.

30 ml rye whiskey
15 ml sweet vermouth
15 ml dry vermouth
Ice cubes

Glass:
Cocktail

Garnish:
A twist of lime

Stir rye whiskey, sweet vermouth and dry vermouth well with ice cubes. Strain into the glass and serve garnished with the lime twist.

EXOTIC

In the event of planning a cocktail party for a special occasion, one might consider serving a diverse repertoire of exotic cocktails such as the Oriental Express and Long Island Tea. These are a departure from the usual one liquor based cocktails and incorporate two or more liquors and a host of flavourings and garnishes.

For eons associated with happy times, all wines and their cocktails reverberate images of parties, celebration, victory and romance. Champagne, the effervescent queen of wines, blends blissfully to form delectable cocktails like French Revolution and Kir Royal.

Lacrime dal Cielo

15 ml brandy (Cognac)
15 ml Cointreau
15 ml wine (Campari)
30 ml grape juice
5 ml sugar syrup
10 ml fresh lime juice
Rosé Champagne
Crushed Ice

Glass:
Champagne Saucer

Garnish:
A pineapple slice and cherry

Blend all ingredients except the champagne. Strain into glass, top with champagne and garnish.

Aaron

Hebrew word for high mountains. Romantically it also means "with love".

30 ml vodka
15 ml crème de cassis
15 ml Baileys Irish coffee cream
15 ml fresh cream
A dash of grenadine syrup
Crushed Ice

Glass:
Champagne Tulip

Garnish:
Cherries

Combine all the ingredients and blend well. Strain the prepared cocktail into the glass, add crushed ice and serve, garnished with cherries.

Negroni

An elegant aperitif liqueur.

30 ml wine (Campari)
30 ml gin
15 ml sweet vermouth
300 ml soda
Ice cubes

Glass:
Highball/Cocktail

Garnish:
A slice each of lemon or orange peel

Pour all the ingredients into a mixing glass alongwith 3-4 cubes of ice and stir. Strain it into the cocktail glass (or highball filled with ice if using soda). Serve, garnished with the orange or lemon peel.

Americano

Actually an Italian drink, it is served as a sunny aperitif.

30 ml wine (Campari)
30 ml gin

Glass:
Cocktail/Highball

Garnish:
A spiral of orange or lemon peel

Stir the Campari and gin together and pour into the cocktail glass (or highball if using soda). Serve, garnished with the orange or lemon peel.

Kir Royal

An exotic champagne cocktail.

150 ml chilled champagne
15 ml crème de cassis

Glass:
Champagne Tulip

Garnish:
None

Pour the crème de cassis first into the glass and then top it with champagne and serve.

Long Island Tea

A disarming name for a tall and potent drink which combines white rum with flavouring such as Contreau.

30 ml tequila
30 ml white rum (Bacardi)
30 ml gin
30 ml Cointreau
150 ml cola
Ice cubes

Glass:
Collins

Garnish:
A slice of orange, a cherry and a mint sprig

Fill the glass with ice and gradually build the drink with tequila, bacardi, gin and then cola. Carefully float the Cointreau on top. Serve, garnished with the orange slice, mint sprig and cherry.

Alfonso

An interesting sweet-and-dry experience.

100 ml champagne (Brut)
30 ml Dubonnet
1 cube sugar
A dash of Angostura bitters
Crushed ice

Glass:
Champagne Tulip

Garnish:
A twist of lime

Pour the Dubonnet, sugar and Angostura bitters and stir. Top with champagne and add crushed ice. Serve, garnished with the lime.

Irish Coffee

A popular nightcap.

45 ml whiskey (Irish)
45 ml whipped cream
45 ml black coffee
15 gms castor sugar

Glass:
Wine

Garnish:
Chocolate flakes

Caramelize the sugar in the glass. Pour whiskey to flamb. Add coffee to it and then whipped cream. Pour a few drops of whiskey on top and serve, garnished with the chocolate flakes.

Buck's Fizz

A long refreshing drink in which the bubbly champagne provides the uplift, while fresh orange juice cushions the falldown.

150 ml champagne
90 ml fresh orange juice

Glass:
Champagne Tulip

Garnish:
A slice of orange

Pour the orange juice into the glass and top it with champagne. Serve, garnished with the orange slice.

Isola de Bachhus

This drink definitely comes from the island of the Greek God of wine, Bachhus.

120 ml white wine (chilled)
15 ml brandy
10 ml kummel
5 ml sugar syrup
10 ml fresh lime juice
A dash of Angostura bitters
A splash of soda
Ice cubes

Glass:
Old-fashioned

Garnish:
A slice of cucumber and a cherry

Pour all the ingredients straight into the glass in sequence, except the ice and soda. Stir, add the ice and then soda. Serve, garnished with the cucumber slice and cherry.

Oriental Express

30 ml dry vermouth
30 ml rye whiskey
30 ml Drambuie
Ice cubes

Glass:
Cocktail

Garnish:
Orange zest

Combine all the ingredients and stir well alongwith 3-4 ice cubes. Strain into the glass, and serve garnished with the orange zest.

INDEX